The Beginner's Guide to Belly Dance

How to Start Your Journey Informed and Empowered!

By Katayoun Hutson

The Beginner's Guide to Belly Dance

How to Start Your Journey Informed and Empowered!

By Katayoun Hutson

Published by Mosaique LLC, 2019

Sterling, VA USA

Copyright © 2019 by Katayoun Hutson
All rights reserved. This book or any portion thereof may not be reproduced or used in any manner whatsoever without the express written permission of the publisher except for the use of brief quotations in a book review.

Printed in the United States of America

First Printing, 2019

ISBN **978-0-9973155-0-9**

Mosaique LLC
Publishing Division

Editing by Lora R. Bates, M.Ed.
Fairfax County Public Schools

Cover photo by Laura Berg

I dedicate this book to all my past students who believed in me as their teacher; to my current students who inspire and motivate me every day; and to my future students, who get me excited about the little things, I cannot wait to meet you!

Contents

Introduction		1
Part 1	**Belly Dance: What It Is; What It Isn't**	
	Myths & Misconceptions	5
	FAQ's (Frequently Asked Questions)	9
	Benefits of Belly Dance	16
	A Brief History of Belly Dance in America	18
Part 2	**Dance & Cultural Vocabulary**	
	General Vocabulary	23
	Belly Dance Styles	25
	Persian Dance & Music	32
Part 3	**Movement Vocabulary**	**43**
	Lower Body Movements	45
	Upper Body Movements	47
	Steps, Pivots & Turns	50
Part 4	**Music Fundamentals & Vocabulary**	**57**
	Essential Belly Dance Rhythms	58
	Melodic Instruments	62
	Legendary Artists	65
	Classic Belly Dance Songs	69
Part 5	**Advice, Etiquette & Encouragement**	
	Class Attire & Footwear	73
	Costumes & Accessories	75
	Classes & Workshops	76
	Shows & Performances	78
Conclusion		79
	Awesome & Amazing Things About Being a Belly Dancer!	
Resources		
	Websites	83
	Books	84

Introduction

When I first started taking belly dance lessons, the internet did not exist. I found my first teacher in the Yellow Pages, the actual printed book. We made our own costumes, and we bought music cassette tapes from mail-order catalogs specializing in Middle Eastern music.

When I first started teaching belly dance, technology had boomed, and so had the popularity of belly dance. While the belly dance industry began to take off in the mainstream, there were very few books, and even fewer available on the mass market. Then belly dance-related resources began popping up on the internet. I was happy to point my students to reliable information that complemented my class lessons.

In addition to those new early resources, I gave brief lectures and created handouts to orient my students to the world of belly dance as a subculture and artistic community. I wanted to empower them with information that would be relevant to them as beginner dancers.

I noticed that students needed information they could digest outside of the dance classroom. They needed guidance to help them make better choices about music, costuming and other products. After two decades of being involved in the belly dance industry, I decided to put all my introductory lectures and handouts in this convenient guide.

Who is this book for?

This book is for you if you are a new belly dancer embarking on your journey. Whether you have started classes or have yet to take the plunge, my goal is to help you make the most of your classes. My wish is that you have a positive experience. I hope this book enhances your class experience. Think of it as a little book of secrets that addresses your specific needs and interests at this juncture. The information I provide will be of immediate and specific interest to you as a beginner dancer, and also a reference point for future research as you grow and develop in your dance studies.

If you are a belly dance teacher who stumbled upon this book, I hope that it inspires you as well, and reinforces your teachings outside of the classroom.

What is covered?

This book includes an explanation of movement vocabulary, musical terms, cultural dance styles, song lists, and many words of advice and encouragement. As you progress in your journey and advance in your dance studies, you will likely seek more in-depth explorations of these topics. I have included recommendations for further reading in the **Resources** section at the end of the book.

I have also included bonus material about Persian dance! As you will discover, Persian dance is not a style of belly dance. However, I have included it because you are likely to encounter the vocabulary of Persian dance and music in your belly dance involvement. While they are two completely different dance forms which developed independently in their respective cultures, many belly dancers enjoy studying these two cultural forms side by side.

How will this book help you?

This book will help you identify the most reliable and credible sources of information and training as you begin and advance in your belly dance journey. Do not spend a dime on any certification program without first reading this book and thoroughly researching the backgrounds of those offering the program. There are many legitimate certification programs, and there are also scam programs. Any program that promises to turn you into a belly dancer in six weeks is simply not a legitimate product. Every professional artist in the industry will tell you that.

While it is important to gather information from different perspectives, information is only as reliable as its source. I hope this book will provide the knowledge base to help you find trusted sources of information and training. My goal is to help you make more informed choices about classes, events and purchases.

How to use this book

Read it cover-to-cover at least once. Study the vocabulary at your own pace. If you are taking classes, you may find it helpful to review terms your teacher uses. While I hope that you enjoy the entire book, I suspect you will find the sections on vocabulary and explanations of industry terms the most useful.

The vocabulary is the collection of terms you will encounter in classes, workshops and online. A working knowledge of the vocabulary is valuable for many reasons. Memory and learning are linked to key vocabulary. Imagine that when you know the name of something, your brain creates a little drawer for that word and that idea. Then, every time you encounter that idea, the brain files everything associated with it in its own drawer. It is then ready to access when you need to recall the information.

Another reason to be diligent about learning the vocabulary of belly dance-related terms is so that you can communicate intelligently with other dancers and musicians. When you are able to understand and contribute to a thought-provoking conversation about the dance, culture and music, it is a great feeling!

***

Part 1
Belly Dance: What it is and What it isn't

Myths & Misconceptions

Common myths and misconceptions about belly dance abound on the internet and in the minds of the general populous. The popular media has fantasized the art of belly dance for the purpose of titillation which has fed these myths for decades. Some are half-truths, and others are just ridiculous and uninformed.

You may find yourself in a position where someone may judge or ridicule your dance activities because they are not educated on the subject. Fear not, the truth is on your side, and it is absolutely more sophisticated and interesting than the myths!

The most common and ridiculous stereotype about belly dance is that it is the "dance of seduction." As a belly dancer, you may come across people in your life who still believe this archaic myth, or other commonly-held misconceptions.

With this book, you will be armed with information to shatter these myths and misconceptions and will be able to handle uncomfortable situations with grace and intelligence.

The following are the most common myths and misconceptions floating around the internet.

MYTH: "Belly dance is the world's oldest dance, over 5000 years old."
Not really. Origin stories which refer to mystical prehistoric and archeological evidence of rituals involving belly dancing are highly disputed. While belly dance derives movement vocabulary from social and folk dance traditions that have been passed down for centuries, belly dance as the performance art we know today is only about a hundred years old.

MYTH: "You don't need any special music for belly dance."
Not exactly. As the popularity of belly dance as a fitness activity has grown, the dance has been removed from its cultural context and many liberties have been taken with musical choices. Belly dance as a cultural art form is performed to traditional and modern Middle Eastern, North African music and sometimes Greek music. You can do whatever you want at home, at the gym or at the club. For performance and legitimate study, the music and culture are as much a part of the dance as the movements.

MYTH: "Belly Dancing makes your belly bigger."
I don't know where this came from, but I have come across it a few times. No, belly dancing does not make your belly bigger, but an unhealthy diet does. Perhaps because belly dancers, who are everyday women just like you, have learned to be comfortable in their bodies, and some of them confidently bare their midriffs revealing their beautiful dancing curves. I suspect that we have been led to believe by the mass media and fitness industry, for a very long time, that there is only

one beautiful body; we have forgotten that beautiful bodies come in all shapes, sizes and colors.

MYTH: "Shakira is the most famous belly dancer in the world."

Shakira is a great dancer, but in the belly dance world, she is not considered the best. She is not really considered a belly dancer. She is primarily a singer, who is of Arab descent. She is famous for incorporating belly dance into her videos and shows, which are choreographed by actual famous professional belly dance stars, such as Bozenka. Shakira's concerts have showcased Arab musicians and renditions of classic belly dance songs, such as Enta Omri, and belly dance-style choreography.

HALF-MYTH: "Belly dance is very easy to learn and lots of fun."

This one is partly true because it IS lots of fun. But if you think it will be easy, you will be highly disappointed. The real art of belly dance is just as demanding as other dance forms. However, one thing that is really unique about learning belly dance today, it is very accessible to all ages, abilities, shapes and sizes. For this reason, it is easy to start learning belly dance. Even if you never plan to step foot on the stage, learn from the start how to do the movements correctly, and you will reap so many benefits. It may not be easy, but if you think you are worth the effort, you might get hooked and never look back.

FACT: "The term 'belly dance' is a misnomer, as every part of the body is involved in the dance."

The term "belly dance" is a misnomer not only because of the reason stated. It is true that every part of the body is involved. The Arabic term, **raks sharqi,** is actually the correct term for what is popularly known as belly dance. It means *dance of the East*, or *Oriental dance*.

Later in the book, you will be introduced to more vocabulary of the dance, music, history and culture. As you become more educated about the art of belly dance, a.k.a. *raks sharqi*, you will be able to intelligently inform others about your dance activities, and hopefully, shimmy your way out of potentially uncomfortable situations.

Often, people appreciate that you took the time to educate them without putting them down or getting defensive. These conversations are important and can be very enlightening. Anytime all parties walk away from the conversation having learned something, it's a win-win!

***

Belly Dance FAQs
Frequently Asked Questions

Q: "Will belly dancing help me lose weight?"
A: Absolutely! As with all forms of physical activity, when practiced regularly in conjunction with a healthy diet, belly dancing can be great for weight loss. You will burn calories, increase flexibility and tone all your muscles.

There are different class formats. A fast-paced format will offer the most cardiovascular benefits. A technique-based class will provide the most strengthening and toning benefits. Be sure to review the descriptions of class formats to determine which one is the best fit for you. If an instructor happens to offer both types of classes, I highly recommend taking advantage of them to give you the benefits of both.

Q: "I am considered plus-size. Can I belly dance?"
A: Yes! Belly dancing does not require a certain body type. Women and men of all shapes and sizes all over the world, belly dance. It is the ideal activity for people who would like to celebrate their bodies while gaining strength, confidence and grace. My personal feeling about size in relation to dance potential is that it is irrelevant.

When I watch a dancer, the first thing I notice is her confidence and grace. The most enjoyable dancers to watch are those who are truly dedicated, and it shows in their joyous passion. I have also seen dancers who would be considered as having the "perfect body" by Western or American standards, but they do not automatically make good dancers. I would never discourage someone from taking belly dance because of his or her body type. And anyone who does, is simply uninformed and knows very little, if anything at all, about belly dance (or anything else for that matter). They are revealing their own insecurities. Do not let them discourage you.

Q: "Is belly dancing hard to learn?"
A: It depends. While gentle and low impact, belly dance is just as demanding as other dance forms. Everyone learns at a different pace and in different ways. It is important to give yourself time to adjust to the movements and develop an ear for the music. Consider your goals. Do you want to learn how to move to the music and feel comfortable on the dance floor or at social events? Or do you want to learn to perform? Each of these goals requires a different mindset, approach and training.

The best advice I can give is this: Enjoy the experience and do not place expectations on yourself in the beginning. You will immediately have more fun when you let go of any pre-conceived notions and expectations. You can figure out your goals as you improve your skills and become more involved in the belly dance community. As you explore your interests, you will discover your strengths. In the meantime, keep dancing and enjoy the journey.

Q: "Can men belly dance?"
A: Yes they can, and they do! Men can enjoy the benefits of belly dancing just as much as women. Belly dance has roots in social and folk dancing of everyday people, which includes men, women and children. While it is more common to see female performers,

there are many prominent male belly dancers and choreographers.

At Middle Eastern social events, you will see men dancing the same movements as women. There are some specific regional dances that are traditionally gender-based, but in general, everyone dances the same way, each with his or her own personal flair.

Q: "At what age can someone start belly dancing?"
A: Any age will do! In the Middle East, girls and women learn belly dance movements almost from birth. Dancing and music are a part of daily life as well as special events. Everyone from toddlers to great grandparents participate.

When seeking classes for your child, the most important thing to look for is instruction that is developmentally appropriate for the targeted age group with respect to mental processing, motor skills and interests.

Q: "Am I too old to start belly dancing?"
A: No way! You are never too old to start enjoying something new! Just be sure to ask questions about the types of classes available to you. Tell your teacher if you have any known injuries, conditions, or limitations, and listen to your body.

Q: "Can I take belly dancing even if I have never taken any dance classes in my life?"
A: Absolutely. There is no prerequisite for belly dancing except a desire to learn and grow. Though some things may come easier if you have dance experience, it is not an indicator of success. Many women who join a belly dance class have never had any formal dance

instruction. Most beginner classes are geared for fun and fitness and you will see a variety of backgrounds, ages, shapes, sizes and abilities.

Q: "When should I start belly dancing?"

A: As with any new exercise program, before beginning classes, you should assess your health risks, needs and interests. Knowing this will help you select a class and teacher that are right for you. You can begin belly dance at any age. Belly dance is actually quite perfect for the first-time adult dancer. There is no age limit.

Some people delay starting classes because they feel the time is not right, ie. new job, stressful job, too busy, not enough money, etc. All of these are legitimate reasons, but excuses will only delay your personal growth and happiness.

With today's technology, there are many options for quality instruction, which can allow you to start dancing right now! Adding belly dance to your life now will actually provide the space you need to better manage the other, less fun, aspects of life. When should you start belly dancing? The answer is now.

Q: "Where can I find belly dance classes?"

A: Depending on where you live, there may be many choices of places to take classes, or there may be only a few. Urban areas will have the most offerings. The venues available in your area can also determine the types of classes offered.

Since belly dance is derived from social and folk dance traditions, there is no standardized way of teaching it. Each teacher will bring her own unique perspective to the dance, and instructional approach will vary from teacher to teacher.

The types of class formats will also vary. For example, if you are primarily seeking to move and have fun, check out dance studios, community and recreation centers as well as health clubs for "fun and fitness" type classes. If you want to learn how to perform, choose a class that focuses more on technique and performance skills. Most teachers of beginners will likely include technique while keeping the class light-hearted and fun. Be sure to read the class descriptions and ask questions in order to select the class best suited for your goals.

There are also many online video classes, DVDs and skype-type classes where you can participate from the comfort and convenience of your home. In-person classes are considered the best type of instruction where you receive hands-on feedback and correction and enjoy the social benefits. However, if going to class is not an option for you right now, online classes and DVDs are a great place to start.

Just keep in mind that if you are not receiving correction and feedback, you could be practicing the movements incorrectly, and it is much harder to break old habits than to learn correctly from the beginning with instructor guidance. For this reason, I recommend working with DVDs and online courses for only a short time, or in conjunction with live in-person classes.

Q: "What should I wear to class? Do I have to show my belly?"

A: Absolutely not. Belly dancing does not require that you expose your midriff. Like other dance forms, belly dance emphasizes a graceful presence that incorporates the entire body. Belly dancing can be practiced in any comfortable exercise attire. Your teacher will provide more information about what she prefers students wear to class. Ideally, class attire should allow your instructor to see your form. You can accessorize with a simple hip scarf. Belly dance is practiced mostly in bare feet. Dance shoes, such as ballet slippers, are usually not required in beginner classes, but they are something you should consider if you continue dance. As you advance in your skills, dance shoes will help avoid injury by making your turns and pivots easier to maneuver.

Q: "What can I expect in classes?"

A: Walking into your first belly dance class is exciting! You may be a little nervous, and that's okay. The first night of class is a chance for the students and the instructor to get acquainted and establish the session's goals. If it is a gym or fitness-based class, the goals are to move and have fun, and there may not be a strong focus on technique or cultural background. Technique and session-based courses often follow a structured format and may incorporate more technique and student correction by the instructor. Whether a drop-in class or an enrollment class, your teacher will probably use a standard class structure, which looks something like this:

1. Greetings and introduction
2. A gentle warm-up
3. Introduction or review of basic moves, followed by new moves or concepts
4. A movement combination, drill sequence or a simple choreography
5. Final activity, cool-down and stretching

Your instructor may talk about her background, training and dance style. During class, she may go around the room and offer correction and encouragement individually to students. Corrections are meant to be helpful. When your teacher takes time to offer feedback, it means that she cares, is paying attention, and knows how to help you make adjustments. Correction is not a personal criticism. It is for your safety and enjoyment, and part of a dance teacher's job.

Teaching styles and curricula vary widely. Different schools and teachers may teach some things differently, or not at all. Don't worry too much about these differences. Each teacher offers something unique from her specific training and interests. As you learn more about dance and teaching styles, and your own goals, you can seek specific instruction with that focus.

Not every teacher is suitable for every student. I usually tell students not to judge the course or the instructor based on one class. After three classes you will have a better idea of how the class is going to work for you. This is not a magic number, but after three classes you know the instructor and class format better, and are beginning to grasp some of the movements. Ideally, you should finish the course in which you are enrolled. It takes time to build a new activity into your regular life routine.

Don't give up! You are worth the effort. An amazing transformation awaits you!

***

Benefits of Belly Dance

You may already be familiar with the benefits of belly dancing, which in part, could be your motivation for wanting to learn. Some of these benefits include:

- Reducing mental stress and muscle tension
- Improving posture and circulation
- Enjoying a positive social and creative outlet
- Increasing core control and flexibility
- Improving brain-body coordination and kinesthetic intelligence
- Increasing mental acuity by engaging both sides of the brain simultaneously
- Improving muscle tone, fluidity and control
- Increasing self-confidence and develop a positive body image
- Gaining cultural knowledge and musical understanding
- Building a strong foundation for further dance study

In addition, there are lesser-known benefits of belly dance that enhance the quality of life.

Physical Benefits and Advantages

The basic movements of Middle Eastern dance and especially belly dance are core-driven, low-impact, and joint-friendly with endless variations to suit different abilities. The movements are naturally adaptable for a gentle body-friendly experience or an intense strengthening and aerobic workout with an infinite variety of combinations to explore!

Increased Life Satisfaction

The belly dance community is an extremely social, supportive and tight-knit subculture which is very welcoming to newbies. Once involved, students are often drawn to the variety of interesting people, both men and women, who make the colorful world of Middle Eastern dance and music go round. There are many styles of belly dance to explore along with the cultural aspects of the dance. Enthusiasts enjoy many social adventures, rare learning experiences, and glamorous performance opportunities, much to the amazement of their friends and family. These experiences and the relationships they build, enrich the lives of dancers for many years.

Mental and Emotional Wellness

It is a well-known fact that dancing and exercise help alleviate the symptoms of depression and anxiety. Belly dance in particular has been noted as a highly therapeutic practice. One possible or additional reason why belly dance is considered more healing and soothing than other dance forms is that the music is highly rhythmic and often described as intoxicating. Music, and particularly rhythms and percussion, have been documented in healing rituals all over the world for thousands of years.

While each person may have their own list of why they enjoy belly dance, it is often not the number of benefits that initially draws them in. What draws anyone to anything? It is a simple emotional awakening in response to something powerful and beautiful....in this case intoxicating music, expressive movements and a wonderful artistic community.

A Brief History of Belly Dance in America

The Art of Belly Dance, or *raks sharqi* (a.k.a. Oriental dance) as we know it today, is only about 100 years old. Derived from folk and social dance traditions, the stage form of raks sharqi became popular in the Golden Era of Egyptian Cinema, from the 1930's to the 1970's. It was parallel to that of the American Golden Age of Hollywood, which made stars of the dancing and singing duo, Ginger Rogers and Fred Astaire. Egyptian Golden Era dancers who appeared in the movies include Samia Gamal, Tahia Karioka, Naima Akef, and Sohair Zaki.

In 1926, Badia Masabni, an actress and dancer, opened the first Egyptian music hall, the Casino Opera, modeled after the cabarets of Europe, which gave rise to the Egyptian nightclub scene. Many of the era's dance stars, such as Samia Gamal, got their start on the Casino Opera stage. These *zaman* belly dancers (dance stars of the Golden Era) whose videos are available on You Tube, are a popular source of inspiration for today's dancers.

The roots of belly dance in America are traced to the appearance of Little Egypt at the 1893 World's Columbian Exposition in Chicago, where showman Sol Bloom introduced the dancing girls of North Africa. He called it "belly" dance, from the French *dance du ventre*, which scandalized the Puritanical audience of the day, who considered the traditional cultural dances an exotic performance of *hootchi kootchi* dancing. The curious crowds came in droves and the scandalous name stuck, as did a distorted reputation of the dance.

Belly dance in America developed through the immigrant populations on the two coasts. Middle Eastern supper clubs popped up all over in the big cities. New York, San Francisco, Boston and Washington, D.C. had lively scenes. Musicians from different countries began playing together and learning each other's homeland music. Dancer entertainers of the day learned the various rhythms and traditional songs spanning the Middle East and North Africa, often including Greek music.

They developed the five-part routine, a compilation of songs from different countries, with different moods, performed for audiences comprised of the Middle Eastern and Mediterranean diaspora, i.e. immigrants from Lebanon, Turkey, Iran, Syria, Armenia, and Greece. This style became known as the American Cabaret style, or Vintage Oriental.

Serena Wilson (1933-2007) was among the early dancers in New York who helped popularize and legitimize belly dance in America as a cultural art form worthy of academic study. She wrote several books, had her own TV show and opened Serena Studios, which continues to operate today.

On the West Coast, we see the origins of the Tribal style. Jamila Salimpour is considered the Grandmother of Tribal style belly dance, and is also credited with a standardized nomenclature of Middle Eastern dance movement vocabulary. With her company Bal Anat, she created a dance and music show for the Renaissance Pleasure Faire in 1968, in which they blended costuming, music and dance traditions of various cultures, carnival style. They had musicians, snake dancers, and the famous Moroccan tea tray dance performed by John Compton (1948-2012). Jamila's folkloric style variety show planted the seeds for the Tribal Belly Dance genre.

Both American Cabaret and Tribal style belly dance are informed by the originating cultures. Though different in expression and presentation, both genres derive movements, aesthetics, costuming and musical inspiration from regional folkloric traditions. Belly dancers of any style and of all levels should not miss opportunities to learn about the dance through its folkloric roots.

In the early days of American belly dance, live musical accompaniment was the norm. Today, it is a rare occurrence, with recorded music of a rich variety available to everyone. Any opportunity to listen or dance to live Arabic music is a special treat and should not be missed.

Through wonderful advances in technology and the important archival work of dance researchers, video footage is now widely available on the internet and documentary DVD's of iconic and pioneering dancers. As you do your own research of dancers and dance styles, be sure to start with these most influential artists.

Egyptian Dance Stars

Aida Nour

Azza Sharif

Badia Masabni

Dina

Fifi Abdou

Lucy

Mona Said

Naima Akef

Nagwa Fouad

Raqia Hassan

Samia Gamal

Soheir Zaki

Tahia Karioka

Pioneer American Dancers

Adriana Miller

Bert Balladine

Carolena Nericcio

Ibrahim "Bobby" Farrah

Jamila Salimpour

Jillina

Morocco (Carolina Varga Dinicu)
Rachel Brice
Serena Wilson
Suhaila Salimpour

***

Part 2
Dance & Cultural Vocabulary

There are many Arabic and Persian words used in the art of belly dance as well as in the belly dance community. I have selected a few words that you are likely to encounter most often in belly dance classes, events and discussions.

Be aware that spellings of Arabic and Persian words will vary because they are transliterated from the Arabic alphabet.

General Vocabulary

Aiwa!: *Arabic exclamation, meaning 'Yes!' or "Yeah!"*

Assaya: *Dance cane used in the women's Egyptian stick dance, raqs al assaya from Upper Egypt, known as the Sa'id region* (pronounced Sah'-EED)

Bedlah: *Two-piece beaded glitzy bra and belt belly dance costume*

Darbouka/Doumbek: *Synonymous with 'tabla,' Arabic drum, shaped like a goblet*

Hafla/Hafli: *Arabic for 'party,' In the belly dance world, it refers to a performance showcasing local students and professional dancers, while promoting community bonding, education and networking*

Khaleegy/Khaliji: *Arabic for 'gulf,' adjective referring to anything from the Persian Gulf region*

Maqam/Maqamat (pl): *Arabic musical mode or scales, each representing a particular emotion or mood*

Tabla (darbouka/doumbek): *Arabic drum, shaped like a goblet.*

Taqasim: *Solo improvised instrumental form. The dancer will often also improvise when dancing to a taqasim piece*

Shamadan: *Candelabra worn and balanced on the dancer's head to perform raqs al shamadan, which is associated with Egyptian wedding celebrations*

Raqs/Raks: *Arabic for 'dance'*

Raks Sharqi: *Arabic for 'dance of the east,' or 'Oriental dance,' the correct and culturally appropriate term for what is popularly known as belly dance.*

Raq'assa/Rakhassa: *Arabic for 'dancer'*

Tahtib/Tahteeb: *Stick used in men's Egyptian martial arts practice and dance performance originating in Upper Egypt.*

Yallah!: *Arabic exclamation, meaning 'Let's go!'*

Zaghareet: *High-pitched yell exclaimed on joyous occasions, and may be heard in lively Arabic musical recordings. At haflas, dancers will zaghareet for each other during performances to show their support and excitement.*

Zills/Sagat: *Finger cymbals, a musical instrument in the Arabic orchestra, and also played by belly dancers, especially those who danced in the U.S. in the 1960's, 70's and 80's. Playing fingers while dancing is not as popular as it once was, though it is still very much an integral part of a serious dancer's training.*

Belly Dance Styles

Raks al Baladi (a.k.a. Folkloric)

Beledi/Balady/Baladi means of *my country*. Each Middle Eastern country has its own unique, traditional form of dance, often thought of as more folkloric or rural.

A baladi Masri, for example, is a dance of Egypt (Masr) and refers specifically to the folkloric style that is unique to that country. Egyptian *Raks al Baladi* encompasses the fellahin (farmers) and Saidi (the Said region or Upper Egypt in the south) dances.

Raks al Baladi is a social celebratory activity that women enjoy in the home and at celebrations, weddings in particular. The *baladi* dance is a more basic form of the stage version of Egyptian *Raks Sharqi*. *Baladi* is more stationary, with hip and abdominal movements being predominant, as well as lots of layering and shimmying.

Baladi also refers to the rhythms commonly used in baladi music. Another name and variation for this rhythm is *maqsoum*. Other rhythms used in raqs baladi are *fellahi* and *saidi* rhythms. *Raks al baladi* is the oldest form of Egyptian solo dance and one of the basic origins of the performance version, *raks al sharqi*. One style of baladi dance that is often incorporated into a *raks sharqi* routine is called *baladi taqasim*, referring to the improvised solo of a melodic instrument.

Egyptian *baladi taqasim* has a specific sequence and development. Egyptian musician Hossam Ramzy, describes the traditional dance this way: *"The Egyptian dancer does not just get up and start to move with great energy. She starts from a slow point and builds up. She is reserved in her first movements and then the music moves to a broken rhythm until it winds up full force in the bigger and livelier movements of the baladi*." Fifi Abdou is considered the most celebrated baladi dancer.

Baladi music, in particular the *baladi taqasim*, which is also known as the baladi progression, often follows a specific structure or pattern. First, with a slow improvisational melody with a *ney*, *oud* or *mizmar*, and in modern versions, the accordion or keyboard. As the piece progresses, percussion accents are introduced in the form of a broken rhythm and there is a call-and-response between the melodic instrument and the percussion instrument, the *tabla*.

The author posing in a baladi dress and holding an assaya, the dance cane used in the women's version of the men's martial arts stick dance, tahtib. Photo by Laura Berg.

The *tabla* then flows into a steady rhythm, *baladi*, *maqsoum* or *sa'idi* rhythm (sometimes all three!), with sections of call-and-response to raise the excitement and anticipation of the dancer's movements.

At the height of the dance, the rhythm and melody become increasingly up-tempo, and the dancer is now moving with wild abandon and lots of shimmies. In the finale of a traditional *baladi taqasim*, the percussion becomes the highlight and builds to a drum solo for an exciting conclusion.

The costume for *raks al baladi* or folkloric style, is a long ankle length fitted dress called a *baladi dress*, or the looser traditional version called a *galabaya*, and a hip scarf. The fabric may be simple cotton or flashy and sparkly. A head band or wrap is also common.

Raks Sharqi

Raks sharqi, is the correct name of the cultural style known as "belly dance," meaning *dance of the East,* or *Oriental dance*. *Raks baladi* refers to the folkloric variations. Both are derived from social, folk and community traditions of the Middle East and North Africa.

Contemporary *raks sharqi* blends the rich and varied musical, dance and poetry traditions of the Arab world to create a highly stylized performance art. The music inspires and propels the dancer, with swooning melodies, dramatic moments, and dynamic rhythms. The dancer becomes the music, interpreting the sounds of the instruments and the layers of the music with her movements and steps.

While many countries such as Lebanon and Turkey have a particular style of belly dance, Egypt is the dominating source of inspiration for dancers in their quest to emulate authentic styling.

Egyptian classical music of the Golden Era continues to be popular among belly dance enthusiasts and world music aficionados. A must in any serious dancer's repertoire, the music of the great legendary artists such as Om Kulthoum, Mohamad Abdel Wahab, Farid al Atrashe, and Abdel Halim Hafez, are standards in classrooms and performance venues worldwide.

Baladi-style dances are often incorporated in the modern Oriental dance set. Sometimes called *magencé*, the modern Oriental dance set is characterized by its rich orchestral sound, modern instrumentation, and rhythm progression of varying tempos, moods and musical flavors within one cohesive piece.

Performing raks sharqi, Washington, D.C. dancer, Janice Nichols, uses the stage name, 'Shukufeh', which means blossom in the Persian language.

Tribal Styles

Emerging from a blend of movements, costuming and aesthetics inspired by various cultural traditions, ***American Tribal Style (ATS), Tribal Fusion*** and other offspring thereof, primarily developed on the West Coast of the United States. Borrowing movements and aesthetics from Arab, flamenco, Persian, and Indian dance styles, ATS is a group improvisational dance which uses a system of cues and transitions to create a unified dance performance on stage, on the spot.

When done well, ATS performance looks choreographed and polished. While dancers must rehearse for many hours to learn the formations as well as detailed movement vocabulary and nuances of the transitions, it is definitely not choreographed. Dancers take turns leading the group, and they must use the designated verbal and non-verbal cue to signal the next transition or movement sequence within 2 to 4 beats (about 1 to 3 seconds, depending on tempo). The music for ATS, like the dance, is folkloric in flavor, a blend of ethnic rhythm varieties, often in a repetitive or simple structure that allows the performance to build from slow, fluid movements to a fast, exciting finale. ATS is always performed as a group.

Costume for ATS belly dance is quite different from traditional raqs sharqi. Like the music and dance, the costume consists of ethnic textiles and jewelry from India, Afghanistan, Egypt and other cultures. One of the most distinguishing features of ATS costuming is the elaborate head adornments (turbans, crowns, flowers, etc.) and long tiered skirts which flare voluminously during spins.

American Tribal Style belly dancers, Wendy Broadway and Tribe Masala (Maryland, USA). Photo by Stereovision.

Tribal fusion is an offshoot of ATS. In contrast to ATS, tribal fusion is more often choreographed, and can be performed by a soloist or a group. There is crossover music from ATS to tribal fusion, though tribal fusion borrows much more inspiration from Western music and dance, such as dubstep, metal and hip hop. Like ATS tribal fusion dance borrows elements from various cultural traditions that includes a wide range of personal tastes and performance styles.

Fusion dance styles are not considered raks sharqi. Dancers who practice fusion styles often have training in various cultural forms which they blend together and it becomes their unique style. Some dancers may their fusion dance style cannot even be accurately described as belly dance. A trained dancer who blends elements and movements of different cultural dance styles for a cohesive performance may be more accurately described as a world fusion dancer.

Belly Dance is a big umbrella term. Not every style of belly dance is a cultural form. It is useful to start learning about established and cultural belly dance styles. As you advance in your dance studies, it is important to learn these distinctions.

In theory, there are specific characteristics associated with each style. However, in the field and on stage, some performances may be difficult to categorize. The labels ***interpretative*** and ***fusion*** dance are often used to describe dance that is not exactly belly dance, but has some belly dance influence.

When you open your mind to the richness and repertoire of movements and music of the cultural forms, you will continue to reap inspiration and enrichment from dance for years to come, as well as learn a variety of techniques to explore your artistic instincts.

***

Persian Dance & Music

Persian dance refers to the traditional dance styles of the country known as Iran (pronounced EE-RAHN). Today, public dancing in the Islamic Republic of Iran is outlawed due to religious restrictions. Dance schools are underground operations, as are performances, usually in private homes. Persian dance as a contemporary performance form, has been developing outside of Iran, for the most part, since the Islamic Revolution of 1979.

This section on Persian dance and music includes vocabulary you are most likely to encounter in classes, articles, videos, and other sources on the internet. While they complement one another in a dancer's repertoire, Persian dance and belly dance are two different forms of dance from different origins.

The author performing Persian classical dance. Photo by Bonnie Austin Stanley.

A common misconception is that Persian dance is a style of belly dance. The fact is, there is no such thing as "Persian belly dance." However, Iranians enjoy belly dance music and performances, especially at weddings and celebrations. In the Persian language (Farsi, not Arabic), they often refer to belly dance as *raghs-eh Arabi*, or Arabic dance, to distinguish it from their own cultural dances.

While Persian dance is not a style of belly dance, it is helpful to know about the dance and music vocabulary, especially if it interests you. This is merely to provide a starting point for further study, and to help you distinguish Persian from Arab dance traditions, origins and styles, such as *raks sharqi* and *raks baladi*.

Persian dance styles are characterized by expressive upper body movements, intricate steps and dazzling spins. There are a variety of Persian performance and Iranian regional styles that share similarities. However, each style has its own unique flavor.

Persian dance is challenging, yet the fluid movements can seem deceptively simple. Beautiful arms, hands, and postures are the hallmark of this style, along with leaning poses and graceful controlled steps, often in intricate circular floor patterns. The main variations in performance styles are characterized by the dynamics of the many upper body movements and nuances.

When referring to the broader category of Persian dance, we often include Iranian folkloric traditions, of which there are many. Some of these regional dances can vary greatly in flavor and aesthetics. In comparing them, they share some similar footwork, styling and floor patterns.

Among Iranians and students of Persian dance, three popular styles are commonly taught and performed: ***Classical Persian Dance,*** the lyrical style which developed from the court dances of ancient Persia; ***Baba Karam,*** the amusing social dance performed at parties; ***Bandari,*** the fiery and energetic folk style which contains elements of African and Arab traditions.

You may be familiar with the exquisite craftsmanship and artistry of Persian rugs. Persians are known for achievements in many areas of visual and performing arts. As in other Persian arts, Persian dance aesthetics are unique and strikingly beautiful.

What is most remarkable about Persian dance in the classical style is the use of the arms, hands and floor space. My primary Persian dance teacher, Dr. Robyn Friend, emphasizes the lady-like and elegant nature of classical Persian dance that is inherent in the movements. The graceful fluidity of the movements is always a goal in practicing technique.

While the sweeping arm gestures and expressive hands are the hallmarks of this style, I would further distinguish Persian dance with the following.

Defining Characteristics of Persian Dance

- Movements are initiated and powered by the core
- Hand and arm movements are fluid and "noodley" - *This is the term Robyn Friend uses, and I think it is a perfect description of some Persian style arm movements that may be stylized differently in other dance forms, such as Flamenco and Oriental*
- Body movements are long and stretchy rather than short and tight
- Movements flow one into the next like Persian writing
- Poses and stillness have energy
- Footwork appears effortless to showcase the upper body
- Arm and hand movements can express abstract ideas and complex emotions
- Dancers can add personal nuances to the movements to express themselves and interpret the music

What I love about Persian dance, first and foremost, is that it connects me to my Iranian heritage, which, in my younger years, I did not appreciate very much. Aside from that, what I love about it is that it is challenging in different ways than belly dance, emphasizing different muscles and focusing on complementary skills, such as upper body, turns and footwork.

While they are so very different, I love Persian dance for the same reasons that I love Egyptian belly dance; that is, the variety of cultural and artistic choices to engage the audience and express yourself with strong powerful movements, or movements that are more subtle and nuanced.

"Salaam", Persian greeting written in Arabic script.

Popular Iranian Dancers

Jamileh

Mohammad Khordadian

Notable Persian Dance Artists & Dance Companies Outside of Iran

Agnes Gagge & Parvaz Ensemble (Sweden)

Banafsheh Sayyad (USA)

Farima Berenji (USA)

Hannah Romanowsky (USA)

Helene Eriksen (USA/Germany)

Helia Bandeh (Netherlands)

Laurel Victoria Gray & Silk Road Dance Company (USA)

Medea Mahdavi (UK)

Miriam Peretz (Israel/USA)

Nomad Dancers (USA)

Pars National Ballet (Canada)

Rana Gorgani (France)

Robyn Friend (USA)

Shahrzad Khorsandi (USA)

Sharlyn Sawyer & Ballet Afsaneh (USA)

Sheila Eghbali (USA)

Troupe Eshveh USA)

***

Persian Music

Traditional Artists (Folkloric & Classical)

Alireza Eftekhari
Faramarz Payvar
Farid Farjad
Hossein Alizadeh
Hossain Tehrani (Percussion)
Kamil Alipour
Kamkars Ensemble (Kurdish Sama)
Keyhan Kalhor
Keyvan Alimohammadi
Madjid Khaladji
Mohammad Reza Shajarian
Shahram Nazeri
Sima Bina

Modern Artists (Fusion & Contemporary)

Axiom of Choice
Azam Ali and Niyaz
Bijan Mortazavi
Earth Drums Ensemble
Farzad Farhangi
Mahsa & Marjan Vahdat
Mamak Khadem
Parviz Panah (RahmanPanah)

Popular Iranian Singers

- Afo
- Afshin
- Andy Madadian
- Arash
- Aryan Band
- Bijan Mortazavi
- Black Cats
- Ebi
- Dariush
- Googoosh
- Jahan
- Hassan Shamaeezadeh
- Heydeh
- Leila Forouhar
- Martik
- Mansour
- Mehrdad Asemani
- Moein
- Morteza
- Nahid
- Omid
- Pouya
- Saeed Mohammadi
- Saeed Shayesteh
- Sandy
- Shahrum Kashani
- Shahram Shabpareh
- Shahram Solati
- Shohreh
- Siavash Ghomayshi

Iranian Regional Dance & Music Styles

Note: Some of these styles are often mixed in with each other due to historical events, migration and changing of geographic boundaries. A clear distinction is not always made, and often debatable between the cultures and ethnicities from which they are derived.

- Azari/Azarbaijani
- Arabi (raqs baladi/sharqi)
- Baba Karam (part of the Jaheli dances)
- Bandari/Abadani
- Bakhtiari
- Baluchi
- Bojnourdi
- Ghafghazi (Azari)
- Ghajari (historical)
- Ghashghai
- Ghassam Abadi/Gilaki/Gilan
- Jaheli
- Kereshmeh
- Kordi (Kurdish)
- Khoram Abadi
- Lezgi (Azari)
- Lori/Lorestani
- Miniature (neo-classical)
- Torki (Turkish)/Torkamon
- Sama (Kurdish spiritual/sufi)

Shateri (part of the Jaheli dances)
Shirazi (city in Iran famous for wine and poetry)
Tehrani (social/party style)

Traditional Iranian Songs

Aha Begoo (Gilaki, from Gilan)
Asmar Asmar (Kordi/Kurdish from Kordestan)
Baba Karam (songs with this title)
Bari Bakh (Azari)
Baroon Barooneh
Bia Berim Dasht/Kooh (classical Persian poetry)
Dokhtar Boyer Ahmadi
Dokhtar Bandari (songs with this title)
Dokhtar Shalabijah
Goleh Sangam/Gol Sang
Layli/Leili (songs with this title)
Mi Juneh Yar (Gilaki)
Rana (Gilaki)
Rashid Khan (Khorasani)
Reyhan (Azari)
Simin Bari
Sari Galin (Armenian/Turkish)
Shaftalooh Foroush
Shazdeh Khanoum

Compilation Albums of Persian Music

Farzand-e-Iran (Child of Iran)

Iranian Traditional & Folk Dance Music

Haft Paykar

Kereshmeh

Masters of Persian Music

Persian Dance Fever

Persian Dance Party

Persian Dances

Raz-o-Niaz

Rough Guide to Music of Iran

Roya (Dream) – Persian Traditional Music

Toh Berakhs

***

Part 3
Movement Vocabulary

The movement vocabulary of Middle Eastern dance is not codified to a common body of knowledge and standards like western dance forms, such as ballet. In its countries of origin, it is usually not taught using the western concepts of structure and technique. Middle Eastern dance is learned as a social dance and those who teach it as a performance art often expect students to do as the teacher does, or what is known as the "follow-the-bouncing butt" format.

If you try different classes with different teachers, you will likely hear different names for similar (or the same) steps and movements. Across geographic lines and dance styles, there is a difference in terminology of movement vocabulary. However, there are some well-known and more established terms that most dancers will be familiar with, such as figure eight and undulation.

I use the most commonly known terms for the movements or steps, along with descriptive anatomical language that can be visualized to describe the motions. Terminology from ballet forms are also used to describe crossover dance concepts and skills.

There are 10 foundational components or building blocks of belly dance. Each teacher will incorporate these concepts differently and at different levels. Depending on the class format, teaching style and dance style, some of these concepts may be explored in the beginner levels or in more advanced levels.

10 Building Blocks of Belly Dance

1. **Isolations:** Muscle contractions
2. **Foundation Movements:** Weight-centered and weight-shifted body articulations
3. **4/4 Shimmies:** Oblique-driven, quad-driven
4. **Steps:** Weight shifts and traveling
5. **Arms:** Movements, transitions and poses or frames
6. **Pivots & Turns:** Foot positions, balance and body carriage
7. **Rhythm, Timing & Coordination:** 3/4 shimmies and step variations
8. **Directions & Dynamics:** Floor patterns and use of space
9. **Layering:** Simultaneous multiple movements and/or dynamics
10. **Choreography and Improvisation:** Musicality and artistry

An *isolation* is a contraction of muscles. By itself, an isolation may or may not be used as a dance move to interpret music. More often, an isolation is a component of a basic movement or articulation. Typically, movement isolations use two sets of muscles, which surround the body part you want to isolate or move.

A *movement or articulation* is a sequence or combination of isolations performed with the muscles in the torso. Movements (and isolations) may be performed with body weight shifted or centered in a variety of dance positions. I use the terms *movement* and *articulation* may be used interchangeably.

A *step* is a shift of weight from one foot to the other, and allows for traveling and other use of space.

Thinking about *movements*, *isolations*, and *steps* as separate concepts will help you build your skills from a strong foundation that incorporate every part of the body.

Lower Body Movements

Lower Body Isolations

Abdominal contraction: A contraction of abdominal muscles: Lower abdominal contraction (pelvic floor) and middle/upper abdominal contraction

Abdominal release: The opposite of a contraction, a release of the lower abdominal muscles. A quick release and contract accent is known as a "belly pop"

Glute contraction: A contraction of the gluteus muscles isolated to one buttock at a time. Popularized in American belly dance by Suhaila Salimpour, glute contractions along with core control, strengthen and sharpen hip movements

Hip Twist: A horizontal twist performed by contracting or stretching the oblique muscles

Hip Slide: A horizontal lateral hip stretch initiated from the obliques. Lengthen the back muscles and shift center of gravity for a hip slide from front to back.

Pelvic Drop: A downward movement of the pelvis releasing the lower abdominal muscles and contracting the lower back muscles

Pelvic Lift (tuck): The opposite of a pelvic drop, executed by releasing or stretching the lower back muscles and contracting the lower abdominal muscles.

Hip Tilt: A tilt of the pelvis, stretching the obliques on one side while contracting on the other, to tilt one hip lower than the other, like a see-saw

Lower Body Articulations and Movements

Horizontal Hip Figure 8: hip slide + hip twist. This move is actually the shape of the infinity sign on the floor ∞, which the hips trace. Direction can be inward (back to front) or outward (front to back).

Vertical Hip Figure 8 up (inward): hip slide + hip tilt up. This movement is also an infinity sign. Imagine tracing this pattern on the wall or mirror with the front of your hips, or on the wall behind you with your buttocks.

Vertical Hip Figure 8 down (outward): hip slide + hip tilt down. Also known as *maya*. This is the opposite of the vertical hip figure 8 up or inward.

Hip Lift: hip tilt upward on non-weighted standing position initiated by contracting obliques with heel off the floor. Variations include hip twist. The accent is on the upward motion.

Hip Drop: Movement starts with hip lift position. The drop is a controlled release through the abs and obliques and can be aided by a gluteus contraction on the opposite (weighted) side to create a percussive movement. The accent is on the downward motion.

Pelvic Circle: This is a dynamic three-dimensional move also referred to as *omi* or *umi* and has two variations. Start with pelvis tucked in and up. Then hip tilt down on R + pelvic drop (release)/hip tilt down on L + pelvic/hip tilt lift R + pelvic/hip lift L. This variation emphasizes the downward motion of the circle (pelvis releases down on the down beat of the music). The other variation starts with pelvis released, then hip tilt up R + pelvic lift/hip tilt up L + hip tilt down R + pelvic drop/hip tilt down L, emphasizes the lift or upward motion of the circle (pelvis pulls up on the down beat of the music). The direction of this move may also be described as clockwise or counter clockwise, though that may be more difficult to visualize since it is not a flat movement.

Hip Circle: Abdominal contraction + hip slide side + hip slide back + hip slide to other side + shift to center/neutral. The knees remain soft, however the pelvis does not tilt as in the pelvic circle. The size of the circle is proportional to how far apart the feet are -- the wider the stance, the better the potential for a larger movement.

Hip Sway: Glute contraction + hip tilt + hip slide or shift of weight side to side.

Hip Shimmy: Fast, alternating hip tilt controlled through the obliques.

Leg Shimmy: Fast, gentle alternating bending and straightening of the knees. This is a loose jiggle of the thighs and buttocks while gently engaging the core without tilting the hips. The knees should never lock in the straightened position during this movement.

Upper Body Movements

Upper body movements and isolations condition the postural muscles and help with developing confidence and grace in arm movements. Ribcage articulations, particularly figure 8s (infinity patterns), help to develop fluidity required in turns, transitions and directional changes. Furthermore, these exercises develop core flexibility that helps a dancer gain full control of her body for dynamic musicality and freedom of self-expression.

Upper Body Isolations

Ribcage slide (chest slide): A horizontal shift of the ribcage side-to-side or forward and back, engaging the obliques, upper abdominal and pectoral muscles.

Ribcage lift (chest lift): A lift of the ribcage using the upper abdominal muscle on the down beat.

Ribcage drop (chest drop): A downward accent of the ribcage using the upper abdominal and upper back muscles beginning with a soft lift, followed by a controlled release on the down beat.

Ribcage twist: A rotation of the ribcage using the obliques and latissimus muscles in the upper back, which brings one shoulder forward while the other shoulder shifts back.

Ribcage tilt: Engaging the obliques to lift and tilt the ribcage, bringing one shoulder higher than the other, like a see-saw.

Shoulder Accent: A sharp movement performed with the pectoral muscles and the trapezius muscles in the upper back. The accent may push the shoulder forward, back or up.

Upper Body Articulations and Movements

Horizontal Ribcage Circle: Ribcage slide forward + ribcage slide to the side, drawing a circle on the floor with the sternum. The movement can be drawn clockwise or counter clockwise.

Vertical Ribcage Circle: Ribcage slide to the side + ribcage lift, drawing a circle on the wall or mirror with the sternum. The movement can be drawn clockwise or counter clockwise.

Horizontal Ribcage Figure 8: Ribcage side + ribcage twist, his movement is a figure of eight (infinity pattern) on the floor with the sternum. The direction of this movement can be back to front (inward) or front to back (outward).

Vertical Ribcage Figure 8: Ribcage lift + ribcage slide, a figure of eight movement (infinity pattern) drawing the infinity sign on the wall or mirror. The direction of this movement can be down to up (inward), or up to down (outward).

Shoulder Roll: A soft rotation of the shoulder forward, up, back and down; or back, up, forward and down using the pectoral and trapezius muscles.

Shoulder Shimmy: Shoulder accents in rapid succession and may also include small twisting motion of the ribcage.

Snake arms: Shoulder roll from the trapezius muscles and pectorals combined with gentle lift and relax of the elbows, alternating right to left. Ribcage twist, slide or figure 8 adds additional layers and texture this movement.

Upper body undulation: Another type of vertical ribcage circle where the sternum draws the circle forward, up, back and down to neutral, ie. chest slide forward + chest lift+ chest slide back + chest drop or release (relax).

Full body undulation: The upper body undulation followed by a lower body undulation in which both movements are performed sequentially. As the upper undulation is about to be completed, the lower body undulation begins.

Steps, Pivots & Turns

All steps can be varied with pivots, level changes, floor patterns, and body movements. When one part of the step is changed, or an element of movement with the body or arms is added, the step can take on new life to suit the mood, flavor, and style of music, as well as the dancer's preference.

To understanding timing and footwork, it is helpful to learn how to count music. Music contains spaces where rhythmic patterns are placed. I call this musical time. In dance, the spaces in music are articulated by numbers, the letters *e* and *a*, and the word "AND." Say the following sequence aloud:

"1 e AND a 2 e AND a 3 e AND a 4 e AND a"
Vocalized as: "one ee and ah two ee and ah three ee and ah four ee and ah"

These counts are used to describe the timing of movements within musical phrases.

Example:

> 2 counts of music is vocalized as, **1 e AND a 2**
>
> 4 counts of music is vocalized as, **1 e AND a 2 e AND a 3 e AND a 4**

Typically, dancers perform steps and movements in half time, full time, double time and for a few movements, quadruple time. Timing is best described by marching in place to a four-count beat.

Half time is stepping only on odd counts (or the down beat) while counting to four, **1 3**. This is a slow march.

Full time is stepping on every count, **1 2 3 4**.

Double time is stepping on every count and the "AND" space, **1 AND 2 AND 3 AND 4 AND**.

Quadruple time is stepping on all the musical spaces, **1 e AND a 2 e AND a 3 e AND a 4 e AND a**. This is a very fast march, resembling running in place.

Steps

Step-Touch: Step with the right foot, then touch with the left foot; repeat, step with left, touch with the right. The count is: 1 = step, 2 = touch

Cross-Point: A variation of step-touch, cross and step the right foot over left, then point or touch with the left foot.

Step-Pivot: Similar to the basic step-touch, this step uses a pivot on the standing foot to change direction. This dynamic can be combined with the basic step-touch and the cross-point to make variations on the weight shift pattern. Step right foot forward, touch and propel with the left to pivot on the ball of the right foot. Pivot direction can be open (outward) or closed (inward).

Step-Close-Step: Also known as the shuffle step or side-step. Take a step to the side with the right foot, close with left, step right again and close but do not step so the left foot remains free. A typical combination is four counts: 1 = step R, 2 = close and step with L, 3 = step R, 4 = close and touch with L; repeat to other side.

Two-Step: Feet are in fourth position (one foot in front of the other). Keep the position of the feet while stepping. There are three main variations of this step. The differences are primarily in the timing tempo of the step.

Variations:

Rock Step (half time): Step R foot forward, L foot back, holding each step for an additional count: 1 step forward, 2 hold/rock, 3 step L back, 4 hold/rock

Flat-Ball (full time): Step right foot flat, step left on the ball, step right on the ball, step left on the ball, ie. flat, ball, ball, ball or forward flat, back ball, forward ball, back ball. In full time, the count: 1 step R, 2 step L. In double time, the count time: 1 step R, AND step L, 2 step R, AND step L.

Tip-Toe (double/quadruple time): Keep the feet very close together, the body very tall and lifted and all the muscles in the thighs thoroughly engaged with soft knees, make small quick steps laterally, keeping the feet very close together, with the lead foot slightly forward. The double-time step counting is spoken as "1 AND 2 AND 3 AND 4 AND" alternating stepping right and left on each utterance.
The quadruple-time step is spoken as "1 e AND a 2 e AND a 3 e AND a 4 e AND a" alternating stepping right and left on each utterance. This step resembles running fast in place.

Three-Step: *step-ball-change, cha-cha-cha,* or *chassé*. Step right, quick step left, step right. Three steps that fit to two beats of music. RLR, LRL. The count is: 1 step R, AND step L, 2 step R.

Four-Step: *scissor step, sharqi step, box step.* This is a 4/4 step with the lead foot stepping forward and back. The count is: 1 step R forward, 2 step L in place, 3 step R back, 4 step L in place. This step can also be performed in double time.

Grapevine: Cross and step the right foot over the left, step to the side with the left, cross and step the right foot behind the left, step to the side with the left, Spoken as "cross front, step side, cross back, step side." Repeat to R with L leading. The count is: 1 cross R over L, 2 step L side, 3 cross R back, 4 step L side.

Pivots and Turns

A pivot for every weight change will create different types of turns. Pivots and turns may be open or closed. An open turn is away from the center of the body. A closed turn is toward the center of the body.

Pivot: a change of direction.

2-step Turn: A pivot on each weight change of a two-step combination.

3-step Turn: A pivot on the first two steps of a three step pattern.

Dancers aim to continually improve their skills no matter their level of experience. Whether it is belly dance or another activity, proper form and muscle engagement can literally make or break your body.

When performed correctly, belly dance is one of most gentle and beneficial activities you can do, no matter your age, ability, size or shape. The movements are inherently low impact and empowering.

When performed correctly, the core-based movements can help strengthen and tone your entire body. When performed correctly, belly dance movements should never hurt, barring any previous injuries or health conditions. Notice the key words are "when performed correctly." In general, a movement is performed correctly when it looks good, does not hurt or cause injury, and interprets the music appropriately.

Body Awareness & Injury Prevention

The best way to prevent injury and create beautiful movements is to avoid common alignment mistakes and engage your muscles correctly.

Eight-point alignment check list:

1. Feet are parallel and hip-bone width apart
2. Weight is centered evenly over both feet
3. Pelvis is neutral (gently engage lower abdominals)
4. Knees are soft (slightly bent), not locked, not overly bent
5. Chest lifted (engage upper abdominals)
6. Shoulders down and relaxed (engage pectorals)
7. Chin is level, neck is long (engage upper back)
8. Elbows are soft, not locked and not bent (engage upper back)

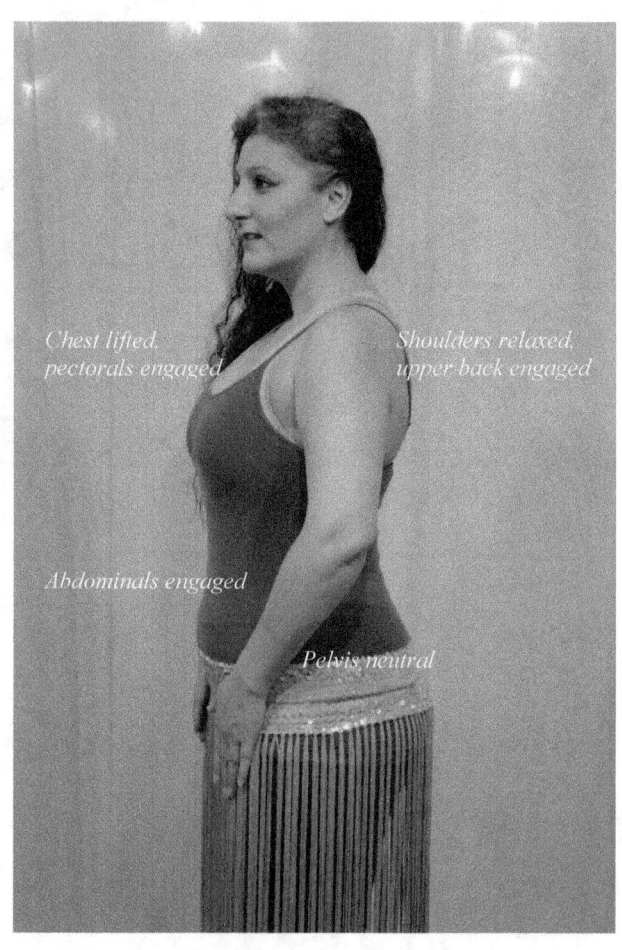

Part 4
Music Fundamentals & Vocabulary

Aiming to understand Middle Eastern music, rhythms and instruments is one of the best goals you can set for yourself. With this essential knowledge, a whole new world of accessible skills and inspiration is at your fingertips….and hips!

As you progress in your studies, look for workshops, DVDs and online music resources to help you form a solid understanding of the music and how it relates to the dance.

Time Signatures

When you see that a rhythm or song is in "2/4" or "4/4" time signature for example, the top number represents the number of beats (or counts) in each measure. A "measure" is the length of the rhythm in musical time. For example, a 2/4 rhythm has only two beats per measure. A 4/4 rhythm has four beats per measure.

The bottom number is important for musicians. The dancer needs to know the top number. Within the timed beats there are accents and pauses. Silence is considered a beat. The most common belly dance rhythms are in 2/4 and 4/4 time signatures. Other popular rhythms are in 8/4, 6/8, 9/8, 10/8.

Essential Belly Dance Rhythms

The rhythms of belly dance music are considered fundamental and are the inspiration for the movements. Used in classical/popular and folkloric music, some rhythms are associated with a specific geographic region. Some rhythms are linked to a specific ritual or cultural tradition. Some rhythms span many different regions, and may even have different names and variations depending on the location or musician.

The rhythms are played on two primary percussion instruments: the *tabla*, a.k.a. *doumbek* or *darbouka* and the *riq*. There are two main accent sounds of the patterns and structures of Arabic rhythms; *Doum*, low resonating sound, and *Tek*, the high sharp sound.

Secondary sounds called *ka* are used to ornament or fill in the empty spaces of rhythmic measure. The letters **D**, **T** and **k** are used when writing out the structure of the rhythms.

Ten essential rhythms are the most popular in modern and traditional belly dance music. Each has a unique flavor and may be associated with a specific type of movement or style of dance. Listening to a variety of Arabic music is a great way to start tuning your ear to the wide range of musical flavors.

Don't worry too much if the structures or patterns of the rhythms don't click with you right away or if you have difficulty telling them apart. Just be aware of how the music and the dance are directly related and in time, it will make sense.

1. Maqsoum (4/4)
Basic rhythm with many varieties, tempos and modes, with a bouncy and steady four-beat structure good for all basic hip movements, back or downward movements, and basic steps. The structure of maqsoum

is the foundation of the most commonly used rhythms in belly dance music.

D T k TD k T
1 A 2 A3 A 4

2. Masmoudi Saghir, a.k.a. "Baladi" (4/4)
Same structure as *maqsoum*, but the first two accented beats are *Doum Doum* rather than *Doum Tek*. The correct name for this rhythm is *masmoudi saghir*, however many American dancers and drummers refer to this rhythm as *baladi*.

D D   T D   T
1 A 2 A3 A 4

3. Sa'idi (4/4)
Egyptian folkloric rhythm and dance style, which includes characteristic hopping steps and bouncy movements. The four-beat structure is similar to *baladi* but with the accented beats reversed.

D T   D D   T
1 A 2 A3 A 4

4. Fellahi 2/4)
The name refers to the *felaheen* or Egyptian farmers. A very fast version of *maqsoum* made to fit a two-beat structure. This upbeat Egyptian folkloric rhythm and dance style has a characteristic forward-back step (similar to the grapevine), and fast articulated hip shimmies, often with traveling steps.

DTDT
1A2A

5. Ayoub (2/4, with variations in 4/4)

Associated with trance and healing rituals, it has a very heavy but simple two-beat structure and is good for isolations, upward or forward movements, and two-step patterns.

D DT
1A2A

6. *Malfuf (2/4)*
A folkloric rhythm that has a rolling sound suitable for many varieties of three-step and two-step combinations. The characteristic step associated with this rhythm is the three-step chassé, which is used often to travel the stage.

D T T
1 A 2

7. *Chiftitelli/Wahda Kabira/Wahda Sonbati (8/4)*
Eight-beat rhythms great for slow and circular movements, figure eights, undulations and lyrical combinations. Often heard as the underlying rhythm of the solo improvised instrument, the musical form called *taqasim.*

D TTD T
1 2 3 4 5 6 7 8

8. *Wahda (4/4)*
With a similar feel to *chiftitelli, wahda* is a four-beat rhythm widely used in Egyptian music, great for slow and circular movements and often heard in the musical form, *taqasim.* Notice the structure is the same as *malfuf,* stretched over four beats instead of two.

D T T
1 2 3 4

9. *Masmoudi Kabir (8/4)*
An eight-beat rhythm associated with classical Egyptian Oriental music as well Arabo-Andalusi music. This rhythm lends itself well to interpretation of a wide range

of horizontal skill-building lessons. Notice the structure is similar to *masmoudi saghir* (little *masmoudi*), stretched over eight beats instead of four.

DD T**D**T T
1 2 3 4 **5 6** 7 8

10. 3/4 or Waltz (3/4)

With the same structure and feel as the western version, this rhythm has a smooth rolling feel making it an easy rhythm to practice three-step combinations, turns and other dynamic movements.

D T T
1 2 3

Melodic Instruments

As with popular rhythms, melodic instruments can be associated with specific movements. While there are no set rules, I like to assign characteristics that capture the feeling of each instrument with specific types of movements.

Accordion– undulations, circles, figure eights, stretchy hip and upper body movements (waves, mischievous)

Brass / saxophone, trumpet – vertical movements (fire, sassy or playful, romantic)

Khanoun/kanun/qanun – vibrating shimmies (earthy or intellectual)

Nay/ney/nai – upper body, veil work (wind, spiritual)

Oud/ud – arms, shoulders, vibrating shimmies (rain, mystical)

Violin – undulations, circles, figure eights, stretchy hip and upper body movements (crying, storytelling)

The rhythm establishes the pattern of movements and steps and can help identify the cultural flavor of the music. When selecting movement vocabulary for a specific piece of music, the melody is actually the main attraction of the piece. The underlying rhythm is a great foundation for portraying the origin and purpose of the piece. However, it is the melody that tells the story. The melody draws us in and evokes our emotions.

The human voice is also considered a melodic instrument. Syllables and intonation in the language and the meaning of the lyrics are all essential elements. For this reason, a dancer should know the meanings of songs she performs.

Popular Middle Eastern Instruments

Nay

Oud

Tabla/Doumbek/Darbuka

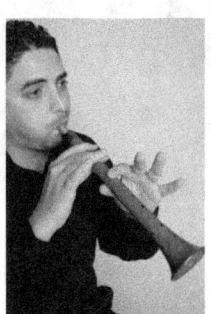
Mizmar

Khanoun

Riq

Folk musicians playing *ney*, *mizmar* and *tabla*, at festival of Egyptian music. Egyptian Cultural Center, Paris, France, 2012.

Legendary Artists

Abdel Halim Hafez
Born: June 21, 1929
Died: March 30, 1977

Famous works include:
"Ahwak" (I Adore You/I Want You)
"Zay el Hawa" (Like the Wind)
"Sawwah" (Wanderer)
"Gana el Hawa" (The Mood Struck Us)

Interesting fact: *He is among the most popular Arab singers of all time. He was also an actor, composer and movie producer. His music is still enjoyed today throughout the Arab world. (Wikipedia.com)*

Farid al Atrashe
Born: October 19, 1910
Died: December 26, 1974

Famous works include:
"Habeena" (Love Me/Love Us)
"Gamil Gamal" (Beautiful Lady)
"Ya Zahratan fi Khayali" (You Appear in My Imagination)
"Awal Hamsa" (First Whisper)

Interesting fact: *He was a singer, composer, actor and virtuoso oud player. He starred in 31 Egyptian musical films, many with the famous dancer, Samia Gamal. (Wikipedia.com)*

Mohamad Abdel Wahab
Born: March 13, 1902
Died: May 4, 1991

Famous works include:
> *"Enta Omri" (sung by Om Kalthoum)*
> *"Enta el Hob" (sung by Om Kalthoum)*
> *"Msafer Wahdak" (Lonely Traveler)*
> *"Zeina" (feminine name meaning beautiful one)*

Interesting fact: *He was the most prolific Arab composer of his time and wrote many songs for Om Kalthum. His orchestrations combined Arabic music with Western musical forms and instruments. (al-mashriq.net)*

Om Kalthoum/Kalsoum/Kulthum
Born: December 30, 1898
Died: February 3, 1975

Famous works include:
> *"Ana Fi Intizarak" (I'm Waiting for You)*
> *"Alf Layla We Layla" (One Thousand and One Nights)*
> *"Enta Omri" (You Are My Life)*
> *"Enta el Hob" (You Are the Love)*

Interesting fact: *"The Voice of Egypt," her songs are known for their melancholy love themes. Though sometimes the music can seem upbeat and happy, they are not happy songs. (Wikipedia.com)*

Popular Singers & Orchestras

In addition to the legendary artists, contemporary artists from the Middle East provide musical inspiration and a variety of musical styles to enhance the dance experience. Famous orchestras are best known for their renditions of classic songs, while contemporary pop stars offer fun, catchy and danceable tunes that are great for practice, performance and listening.

The following are a few artists to look up when searching for belly dance music.

- Al Ahram Orchestra
- Amr Diab
- Baligh Hamdy
- Cairo Orchestra
- Eddie "The Sheik" Kochak
- Fairouz
- George Abdo & The Flames of Araby Orchestra
- Gizira Band
- Hakim
- Haifa Wehbe
- Hossam Ramzy
- Mario Kirlis
- Mohomed Mounir
- Mokhtar al Said Orchestra
- Moustafa Amar
- Najwa Karam
- Nancy Ajram

Natacha Atlas

Saad

Sabah

Sami Nossair Orchestra

Salatin al Tarab Orchestra

Setrak Sarkissian

Tarkan

Upper Egypt Ensemble

Wael Kfoury

Warda al Jazairia

Zamalek Musicians

***

Classic Belly Dance Songs

One of the most fun aspects of belly dance is dancing to songs that take us on a journey. Funky, sassy, melancholy, or uplifting, classic songs inspire movement, evoke emotion, and awakens our artistic expression.

There are many songs considered "must-know" for belly dancers. These songs have significant lyrics and dancers should make an extra effort to learn what they mean in order to learn how to dance to them.

Classical Egyptian songs by the legendary artists are especially popular and essential to know. Some of the songs used for belly dance performances are short introductions of a longer song, often 45 minutes to one hour in length. These introductions do not have lyrics. Also, some of the dance pieces are not introductions, but are the actual song with lyrics, even if it is an instrumental version.

Additionally, you might find there are versions of a song in different languages and cultural traditions, and they may be known by different titles.

You don't need to know all the intricacies and distinctions until you become a serious dancer or start performing. Just being aware they exist will give you a head start when you are ready to dig deeper into belly dance music appreciation and study.

As you gain more dance experience and training, ask questions about the music used in classes and workshops. Learning about the music is one of the most empowering and enjoyable experiences of learning the art of belly dance.

The following is a very short list of classic belly dance songs often heard in classes, workshops and performances. I have selected a few of the most popular titles.

There are many versions of these songs available. Plug them into a search engine and have fun listening, exploring, analyzing and dancing.

Alf Layla We Layla (One Thousand and One Nights)

Ala Nar (On Fire)

Ana Fi Intizarak (I'm Waiting for You)

Aziza (*a woman's name*, Precious)

Bahlam Beek (I'm Dreaming of You)

Batwanis Beek (You Are Always With Me)

Bir Demet Yasaman (A Bunch of Yasmin)

Daret al Ayam, aka: W'Darat al Ayam/W'marat al Ayam (And the Days Pass)

Enta Omri (You Are My Life)

Fakkarouni (They Reminded Me)

Habeena (Love Us)

Habibi Ya Eini (My Darling, My Eyes)

Haramt Ahebak (I Give Up Loving You)

Lamma Bada Yatathana (When She Begins to Sway)

Layla (Written for Layla al Jaza'iyra)

Lessa Fakr (Do You Remember?)

Leylot Hob (Love Night)

Misirlou (Egyptian Girl)

Tamr Henna (Henna Flower)

Rompi Rompi, a.k.a. Çadarimin Ustunü (Rain Dripped on My Tent)

Tahtil Shibbak (Under the Window)

Ya Ein Moulaytein (Two Girls By the Spring), aka: Shashkin (Confused)

Zeina (*a woman's name*, Beautiful)

Zey al Hawa (Like the Wind)

***

Part 5
Advice, Etiquette & Encouragement

In this final section, I want to offer you educational tidbits and helpful hints of some of the customs and practices you may encounter in the belly dance world. Whether long-standing traditions unique to the belly dance community, or borrowed from other industries, these are practical tips gathered from many years of experience. While each community will have its own standards and traditions, there are some things that are considered common to most belly dance communities.

Class Attire & Footwear

You already know to wear comfortable, form-fitting exercise attire to class. Many studios and instructors may not allow coin or beaded hip scarves. Coin scarves are very noisy, which can be distracting. Even the best quality beaded scarves will shed beads and coins onto the floor after wear and tear, which can cause injury if stepped on.

Resist the urge to buy novelty belly dance costumes or accessories for class. Forego the heavy beads and coins and opt for bright colors, sparkly fabrics and fun patterns instead. Class attire can be fun without the distraction of heavy or unnecessary accessories; it should be simple, comfortable and allow for movements to be easily seen.

Footwear is also something to consider. While Middle Eastern styles are relatively joint-friendly, all dancers need to consider proper footwear, especially as the frequency, level and commitment of dance classes increases. Proper dance footwear is not only important for proper execution of steps, it is imperative for dance longevity.

Student Becky Lou with the author in suggested class attire. Photo by Laura Berg.

Dance shoes can help prevent damage from repeated stress on the knees and hips, especially during pivots and turns. Even if pivots and turns are not integral in your class repertoire, knee pain can develop over time from tiny stresses that torque the knee even with the most basic steps.

A common misconception is that dance shoes are expensive. This may have been true years ago, but not today. Dance shoes are very affordable, and often cost the same or less than their counterpart street shoes.

The brand of dance footwear is less important than the comfort and style for your dance discipline. For all styles of Middle Eastern dance for both adults and children, a basic leather or canvas ballet slipper works well. Dance sneakers are also a great option, especially if you have special needs for your feet or knees.

The most important factors in selecting a dance shoe are sizing and fit. Pay attention to the sizing charts and read reviews if available. Each brand is different. Some brands run small, others run a bit big. It is helpful to read reviews from others. Remember that leather slippers will stretch and form to your feet; it is normal for them to feel a little tight when they are brand new.

Invest in proper dance shoes. You will enjoy your classes more, get more from your dance experience, and you may even feel more confident and capable as a dancer.

Costumes & Accessories

As a beginner student, you don't need to invest in performance costumes. Your first performance will likely be in a student or community event under the direction of your teacher. There are a variety of costume styles available. Costume styles are also associated with specific cultural and performance styles.

When a performance opportunity arises, your teacher will provide guidelines and instructions on the required student costume that is best suited for the theme and style of the piece. Until then, you do not need to purchase a costume.

Like the music, belly dance clothing and costumes are a big draw to the dance. Depending on the local belly dance scene, you may have opportunities to see professional dancers performing in dazzling costumes. If performing is your goal, when you are ready, you will hone skills at appropriate student events, such as haflas, and with appropriate student costumes.

I have a very important piece of advice for new dancers about costumes, clothing and accessories.

Don't spend more money on costumes than on dance lessons.

When a dancer takes the stage in an exquisite costume, my excitement begins to build in anticipation of seeing the dance. At that moment, I hope that I am not disappointed. Invest in your dance training now and moving forward. You don't want to be the dancer whose costume is the only memorable part of the performance.

Classes & Workshops

Class and workshop etiquette creates a positive experience for all participants.

Rotate rows: In large classes and workshops, the instructor will often rotate the rows so that everyone has a chance to be up front at some point during the class. Do not hog the front, move back when instructed. Look around to see who is in your row and be aware of your spacing.

Listen to the instructor: When you pay for instruction, you expect the teacher to be prepared and offer a good learning experience, right? You, the student, are expected to pay attention and do your best. Even if you think it's too easy, too hard, or weird, or uncomfortable, trust that the teacher has a plan and it will all eventually make sense.

Sometimes you think you know the move, but the instructor may be demonstrating a whole new way of thinking about it. Listen and follow directions as if you are doing it for the first time. You might just have a breakthrough.

Exception: *If you know a certain type of move or position isn't good for you because of an injury, or you experience pain when performing it, stop. Ask for a modification. And if none is available or if there is no opportunity, just don't do it. If you can, let the instructor know. Don't risk injury.*

Get out of your comfort zone: In order for growth to happen, you have to be willing to step out of your comfort zone. Take a risk and open yourself to new and challenging experiences. It is okay not to be good at something, especially in the beginning. In fact, if you want to succeed, it may be necessary to struggle for a while, and even fail a few times.

Thank your teachers and mentors: Belly dance teachers are some of the smartest, most creative and hard-working people you will ever have the privilege of knowing. It takes countless hours, buckets of sweat and thousands of dollars to train well in dance, and even more to learn how to teach. Not everyone who has dance knowledge, wants to teach. Be sure to let your teachers know that you appreciate them. A sincere "thank you" is a good start.

Shows & Performances

Being a good audience member: Smile at the dancer, especially if you know her, clap and *zaghareet*. Belly dance shows are not the ballet. The audience and dancer are expected to interact. Sometimes audience members may join the dancer on the dance floor! All of it is meant to be a joyous and celebratory experience.

Tipping the dancer: It is perfectly appropriate to tip the dancer. Let her show you how to do it and where to put the bills. Some dancers prefer not to be touched or tipped in their costume, even by women. In many cultures, bills are thrown over the dancer's head in what is known as a money shower.

Maintaining the Mystery: There is a unique allure to belly dancers, regardless of their age or experience. Performing in public, even as a student, can sometimes garner unwanted attention. Many dancers take stage names. A stage name can be a fun way to get into your dance persona, or as my troupe-mate Sitara says, your superhero identity. A stage name can also protect your privacy. At *haflas* and shows, dancers wear a cover-up, a caftan-like dress, over their costumes when they are not performing. This helps protect your costume, and it also maintains the mystery of your stage persona.

***

Conclusion

I want to leave you with some words from the wonderful belly dance community. They are students, much like you, as well as teachers and professional hobbyists. It is the community that makes the experience of dance even more powerful, enjoyable and transformative.

Whether it is taking your first class, returning to classes, or stepping up your dance involvement, this is what you can look forward to when you take the next step in your belly dance journey.

Awesome & Amazing Things About Being a Belly Dancer:

"As you learn to isolate muscles, you become intimately connected to your own body. It's an entirely different level of physical self-awareness that causes you to be more in tune with the natural cycles and changes in your body." Leilah Moon – Rockville, MD

"Belly dance opened me up to parts of the world I knew little about." Theresa Swain - Badin Lake, NC

"You learn how to feel beautiful and strong, regardless of your age, gender or physique." Heather Anne - El Dorado Hills, CA

"You learn to embrace your inner Goddess and outer roundness!" Molly Renne - Eugene, OR

"Belly dance saved my life and for the first time, I thanked God for being a woman." Bel Jones - Mechanicsburg, PA

"Best thing about being a belly dancer: freaking people out when you roll your stomach! And then of course the high from performing." Phanessa Hartley - Winnipeg, Manitoba, Canada

"You never know where the dance will take you; trips abroad or girls' night out raising money for charity." Caroline Shinydancer – Derbyshire, UK

"Dancing is a great way to express all your emotions and letting people into your inner soul. Also as a teacher getting to work with amazing women!" Alexia Smith - Knoxville, TN

"Dance is the physical expression of your inner feelings come to life." Amy Byrum-Strickland - Chesapeake, VA

"Unleash your feminine energy, unveil your beauty within, be the Love that you are." - Solitaire Darling - Kuala Lumpur, Malaysia

"It has art and creativity and athleticism and acting, all in one. At its best, belly dance is just plain MAGIC. And transformative." Shakira Al Fanninah - Columbus, OH

"It's all about women's empowerment- embrace your Inner Goddess!" Shonne Denou - Ballston Spa, NY

"Through dance you have the ability to discover incredible amounts about yourself personally, professionally, and socially. You just have to take the challenges, listen to the advice, believe in it all, and allow yourself to feel." Ayperi Leyla - Gainesville, VA

"Belly dance satisfies my inner me, and I can let go of anything that's bothering me. When I dance with our group of beautiful ladies I can't help but smile from ear to ear. Over the last 8 years we've all become beautiful soulmates." Kerstin Boyd - Warkworth, Ontario Canada

"Belly dancing is the only way I've found of expressing what I'm thinking or feeling." Eleanor Gaywood – Sheffield, UK

"To Dance is to Live. To Live is to Dance!" Alexandria – Beckley, WV

"I'm not mom, or Mrs., or ma'am, or a coworker, daughter or fixer of problems - when I dance it's just me being me!" Peg Tigue Hain - Woodbury Heights, NJ

"Dancing is life; the rest is just details!" Penny O'Keefe – Filer, Idaho

"Belly dance is my favorite subversive activity." Denise Gilbertson - Eugene, OR

"Thank you belly dance for making me feel beautiful, powerful, and strong." Veronica Cargill - Bakersfield, CA

"Sharing a love of dance, music, costumes, and fantastic experiences, with my amazing Sahara Sister friends, without ever being judged, or put down, no matter how I'm feeling about myself!" Rachel Terry – Chippenham, Wiltshire UK

My wish for you, as it is for all of my students, is that you find as much joy and fulfillment in this beautiful art as I and so many others have. Even if it seems hard, I want you to know that the journey is much more empowering, interesting and transformative than the destination.

I want to inspire you to take the plunge and join a live belly dance class (if you have not already), and to keep at it and believe in yourself. I want to encourage you to keep learning, and continue to challenge yourself. I hope that I have done that. You are worthy and deserving of this amazing experience. Enjoy every moment.

****

Resources

Websites

All About Belly Dancing! – by Shira
shira.net
The very first and longest running comprehensive website dedicated to the art of Middle Eastern dance, this site has articles on a vast array of topics from dancers all over the world. Shira also reviews many products, such as DVD's and books. There are many song translations, an invaluable resource for dancers of all levels.

Daily Bellydance Quickies (videos and blog)
shes-got-hips.com/learn-to-dance/daily-belly-dance-quickies
Mahin sends tips, tricks and advice via her blog and quickie videos. Geared for everyone involved in belly dance, each edition has a different theme to cover the spectrum of belly dance-related topics.

Gilded Serpent – by Lynette Harris
gildedserpent.com
The first internet magazine for belly dance enthusiasts, this e-zine is dedicated to news and information about Middle Eastern dance, music, culture and history. Articles are written by dancers and experts from all over the world on a vast array of topics, trends perspectives.

Morocco's Meanderings – Published Articles
casbahdance.org
Carolina Varga Dinicu, considered the leading authority and influential figure in the Middle Eastern Dance community, shares articles based on her extensive knowledge and real life experiences.

Books

The Art of Persian Dance, by Shahrzad Khorsandi.
ISBN: 978-0692364635
This is the first book published to establish a formalized pedagogy which encompasses the foundational principals of Persian dance technique and aesthetics. Rich with photographs and illustrations, the book details Persian dance positions, concepts and movement vocabulary.

Bellydance: A Guide to Middle Eastern Dance, Its Music, Its Culture and Costume, by Keti Sharif.
ISBN: 978-1741143768
This is a wonderful lush book that offers cultural and historical information about belly dance as well as music and movement vocabulary. This is a very easy read with many photographs.

The Belly Dance Reader, by Lynette Harris.
ISBN: 978-0615735597
This book is an anthology of essays from dancers and scholars in the worldwide belly dance community. It includes artwork and articles addressing a wide range of subjects, such as music topics, how-to's, history, culture, dance styles, and perspectives.

Images of Enchantment, Edited by Sherifa Zuhur.
ISBN: 978-9774244674
While not specifically about dance, this is an academic book that explores the arts of the Middle East. Comprised of 18 articles and essays about music, dance, painting, and cinema, it delves into the societal and cultural nuances that shape the perception of art and artists.

Looking for Little Egypt, by Donna Carlton.
ISBN: 0-9623998-1-7
This book is a researched account of the legendary Little Egypt, her famous appearance at the 1893 World Exposition in Chicago, and the role Sol Bloom played in bringing Oriental Dance to the United States.

The Soul of Belly Dance in Color: History and Culture, by Mezdulene Bliss, Shira Elliot, and Morocco (C. Varga Dinicu).
ISBN: 978-1502549747
This book explores the music, culture and history of belly dance. Three prominent experts share their research and experiences.

A Trade Like Any Other: Female Dancers and Singers in Egypt, by Karin van Nieuwkerk.
ISBN: 0292787200
This book attempts to shed light on the cultural notions which perceive female entertainers as low class, while a revered few achieve legendary status. It is considered a well-researched work which explores in depth the Golden Era of Egyptian film, music and dance.

You Asked Aunt Rocky: Answers & Advice About Raqs Sharqi & Raqs Shaabi, by Morocco (C. Varga Dinicu).
ISBN: 978-0983069041
Affectionately known as "Aunt Rocky" in the belly dance community, Morocco answers questions originally posted on the the MED-List, the first internet belly dance forum. With over 50 years of research and experience, this encyclopedia of a book is a treasure trove of information and advice.

About the Author

Katayoun is a master teacher, author and national presenter. She specializes in a broad range of Middle Eastern and North African dance styles with a knack for creative drills and choreography.

A former classroom educator, she has taught weekly classes to a diverse array of students since 1999, accumulating nearly 10,000 instructional hours in the studio and the classroom.

For two decades, she served the Washington, D.C. area as a respected leader in the dance community, earning a reputation among students and colleagues as a passionate and dynamic instructor, performer and mentor. Her methodology highlights the aesthetics of cultural dance with a body positive approach aimed for dancers of all ages and abilities.

Katayoun is founder of the Mosaique Collaborative (formerly known as Mosaique Center for Cultural Arts) in Sterling, Virginia. Her book, *Oriental Dance Curriculum, Beginner to Multilevel: A Complete Guide for the Belly Dance Teacher* is available at book retailers worldwide.

KatayounDance.net

Twitter.com/KatayounDance

Facebook.com/KatayounDancer

Dance while you can.

www.ingramcontent.com/pod-product-compliance
Lightning Source LLC
Chambersburg PA
CBHW070436010526
44118CB00014B/2067